British Railways
STANDARD CLASS 5

British Railways
STANDARD CLASS 5

David Clarke

Ian Allan PUBLISHING

Front cover, top: No 73085 is seen on 5 September 1965 passing Battledown flyover, just to the west of Worting junction where the Southern's Bournemouth and West of England lines diverged. *Colour-Rail (381329)*

Front cover, bottom: The 73124-154 series was built with Caprotti valve gear. No 73136 is on the Saturdays-only 17.50 Derby–Rowsley at Lea Wood Tunnel in July 1963. *Colour-Rail (BRM814)*

Rear cover: No 73086 at the head of a short consist of milk tanks is seen at Wimbledon on 29 May 1963. *R. E. Ruffell*

Previous page: No 73024 is seen in green livery complete with red route availability indicator below the number. This locomotive spent its entire working life on the Western Region with two spells at Shrewsbury as well as Bristol, Gloucester, Llanelly and Oxford. *Hugh Daniel / Colour-Rail (BRM2141)*

Above: On 3 January 1966 No 73089 is seen shunting in Clapham yard carriage sidings. *R. E. Ruffell*

First published 2012

ISBN 978 0 7110 3392 4

Published by Ian Allan Publishing

an imprint of Ian Allan Publishing Ltd, Hersham, Surrey, KT12 4RG.

Printed in Malta.

Distributed in the United States of America and Canada by BookMasters Distribution Services.

Visit the Ian Allan Publishing website at www.ianallanpublishing.com

Contents

Acknowledgments

I am old enough to have seen many of the Standard Class 5s in traffic, and was fortunate to have been pulled by a number of the class on passenger trains as my local shed (Shrewsbury) had a large allocation of the class, used on trains from Shrewsbury to Stafford and Shrewsbury to Wolverhampton which I travelled on regularly. In my eyes the class had a more elegant look when compared to the far more common LMS 'Black 5s' and the use of the lined green livery on some examples only enhanced their appearance. When pushed however they could produce a real 'bark' from the exhaust and more than matched their contemporaries, the 'Black 5' and the 'Halls'.

The Standard 5s from a detail point of view are deceptively complex with many of the detail changes being very subtle and not always easy to spot in photographs. The Engine History Cards have been analysed but as with many other classes, the cards suffer from not being fully updated from the early 1960s onwards so many of the later changes (such as speedometer and tender changes) were not officially recorded. So to identify many of these latter changes I have used an extensive collection of photographs and observations from such as the *Railway Observer*. Where I have used previously published lists for changes and variants I have validated this with photographic evidence and where the photograph contradicts the published data I have not used the published sources. In the course of doing the research for the book I came across a number of contradictory statements, so if there are any errors they are mine not a simple reiteration of 'facts' from an unknown source.

The class has surprisingly not been well covered in book form compared to many other classes but the RCTS book on the BR Standard 4s and 5s is very detailed with a considerable amount of official data, so the obvious question to ask is 'what does this book have to add to the story' beyond the obvious one of having colour photographs? I have tried to summarise all the detailed changes in a compact format so that when viewing a photograph the reader should be able to identify any changes made to that particular locomotive. Whilst the RCTS book has considerable official data in it, I have tried to validate this by extensive analysis of hundreds of photographs and this has produced additional information not always officially recorded. The objective of this book is to show to the reader the detail variations within the class in an easily understandable form and, where possible, tables have been used to summarise the as-built configuration and allow easy reference, and the text describes subsequent changes. The photographs have been chosen to show as many of the possible variations through the class.

Producing a book is not a solitary process; a number of people have provided help and assistance. Thanks to Norman Preedy for digging through his archive of black and white photographs for items not used before and to John Jennison for his help and in checking the text.

There are also a number of excellent websites which are listed at the end of the book. As with all these Societies they deserve your support to keep the locomotives running.

David Clarke

Recommended reading:

BR Standard Steam Locomotives Volume 3. RCTS. This volume covers all the BR 4-6-0s, the Standard 5s and the Standard Class 4 in some considerable depth and is thoroughly recommended.

The Power of the BR Standard 4-6-0s. Gavin Morrison, Ian Allan 2003. A general photographic book on both classes.

British Railway Standard Steam Locomotives. Edward Talbot, Oxford Publishing 1982. A good photographic review of all the standard classes.

Locomotive Panorama Volume 1. E. S. Cox, Ian Allan 1966. This gives an authoritative insight into the development and production of the standard classes from someone who was intimately involved in the process and decision making. Strongly recommended.

The Standard Arthurs. Camelot Locomotive Society 1981. (ISBN 0950776106). A small booklet compiled by P. W. Gibbs covering the named examples on the Southern Region. It also includes some reminiscences of Peter Smith who fired and drove the class on the S&D and then the Southern Region. This is an excellent booklet and shows that when driven and fired properly they were an excellent locomotive and more than matched the 'Black 5', 'B1' and 'Halls' and in some drivers' views were as good as a Bulleid Pacific.

From Barry to Bluebell. Camelot Locomotive Society 1996. (ISBN 09507761 2 2). A brief study of the class but mainly the story of No 73082 *Camelot* and its restoration on the Bluebell by the society.

LMS Locomotive Profile No 7 Caprotti Valve Gear Engines. Hunt, Jennison, James and Essery, Wild Swan 2006. Part of the excellent Wild Swan series on LMS classes, it details the development of Caprotti valve gear used on the LMS 'Black 5s' and how the final two locomotives in the class were effectively test beds for the Caprotti valve gear used on the BR Standard Class 5.

Introduction

Whilst it can be considered that the
BR Standard Class 5 locomotive was essentially
a copy of the LMS 'Black 5', this would be
a considerable over-simplification.

With the formation of British Railways (BR) on 1 January 1948 a new strategy was required for the forward development of motive power. The issue could be distilled into two options:

1. Allow the newly formed regions (based very much on the companies of the former Big Four) to continue to design and build their own locomotives, independent of the other regions.

2. Develop a range of 'Standard' locomotives that could run on any of the regions and incorporate best design practice, not only from within the UK but from the rest of the world, particularly from the USA. This standard range would be the only new build allowed until electrification could commence. The development of steam power was seen as a stopgap measure until major electrification schemes could be implemented. At this point in time dieselisation was not an option.

The decision was made that the preferred option would be to design a range of standard steam locomotives and to stop building any of the former railway company designs. One of the principal reasons behind this decision was to reduce the cost of both building and operating. In the postwar period there was a recognition that there would be shortages of labour in the area of locomotive maintenance. New designs should incorporate features that would make servicing and maintenance easier and

lengthen the mileage between component replacement or repair.

However, it would take time to design and build these new standard locomotives and for a short period between 1948 and 1951 some existing designs continued to be built to fill the gap before the new classes became available. Examples of former Big Four classes built in this way include, LNER 'A1' (21 built), LNER 'A2' (14 built), ex-LMS 'Black 5' (40 built), GWR 'Castle' (30 built) and GWR 'Hall' (58 built). A total of 1,538 locomotives of the Big Four designs were built after the formation of British Railways before any of the BR Standard classes were introduced.

As a precursor to the production of any standard designs and to assist in the design process, locomotive trials were arranged in 1948. The most modern locomotives in a number of categories were run on other regions and comparisons made on some key criteria, such as average and maximum power, and also coal and water consumption. The exchanges produced some interesting data with some classes doing much better than expected and much of the information was incorporated in the new designs.

The list of standard locomotives had four completely new designs (the 'Britannia', 'Clan', 'Duke of Gloucester' and the Standard 4), four new designs based on existing types, including the Standard Class 5 (based on the 'Black 5') and four using existing designs with only minor modifications. The decision on which design to

Above: No 73086 *The Green Knight* at Nine Elms. The background to the nameplate is painted black. On the smokebox door are the additional brackets for the Southern Region route indicator disks or lamps. *Author's collection*

Right: The driver of No 73155 waits patiently for something to happen. The battery box for the AWS can be seen below the cab, as can the upper part of the Smith-Stone speedometer drive. *Ian Allan Library*

Below: No 73020 displays the care-worn condition of most of the class in 1967. Note the two lifting brackets on the cab roof fitted to locomotives in the class on the Southern Region. The original style cab handrails are visible. *Ian Allan Library*

73020

proceed with first .was driven by operating considerations. The most urgent need was for a Class 7 locomotive to improve services on the Great Eastern section of the Eastern Region, so the 'Britannia' became the first of the standards entering service in 1951.

There are many who questioned the wisdom of designing a new range of locomotives rather than continuing to build designs from the former companies, but this is not the *raison d'etre* of this book, my role is to detail what was built, not to challenge why.

Above: No 73002 displaying a 17A Derby shed code, to which shed it was allocated. The locomotive was allocated to Derby twice: in 1951 when first built (for five months) and again in January 1952 for another 10 months. The locomotive was finally withdrawn in 1967 from the Southern Region.
No 73002 was scheduled to have been the first of the class to be fitted with a double chimney. However, this was never fitted.
Ian Allan Library

CHAPTER ONE

Design

Under the direction of R. A. 'Robin' Riddles the design
of the BR Standard classes was intended to take the
best practice not only from the previous companies
but also from foreign locomotive design.

In 1948 the newly formed British Railways (BR) set up a design team under R. A. 'Robin' Riddles to design and build a range of 'standard' steam locomotives to fill the gap before the railway network was electrified. The design of the BR Standard classes was intended to take the best practice not only from the previous companies but also from abroad. During World War 2 some of the features of the US-built 'S160' class 2-8-0 attracted some attention as 390 of the class were operating on the British network allowing them to be studied in detail before they were moved to Europe following the invasion. These locomotives had a wide firebox over the rear trailing axle, a high running plate and incorporated the use of a rocking ash grate and self-cleaning smokebox to make ash disposal easier.

In addition to having a US-built locomotive to study at close quarters, at the end of the war a number of senior engineers from the LMS and LNER visited the USA to study railway practice and nine of that country's leading railroad companies were visited.

These US-built locomotives considerably influenced a number of LMS designs (such as the 2-6-0 Ivatt Class 4 and the Ivatt-built Class 5) which incorporated a rocking grate, high running plate, self-cleaning smokebox, manganese bearings and roller bearings. Many of these features subsequently appeared on BR Standard designs.

Before any firm designs were drawn up the 1948 locomotive exchanges were run and this initially led to consideration of a Class 5 Pacific following the better than

expected performance of a Bulleid Light Pacific. However after further analysis, the better traction and lower cost of a two-cylinder 4-6-0 won the day. In the light of the subsequent disappointment over the Class 6 Pacific ('Clan' class) this was definitely the correct decision, as all the regions had a lot of collective experience with two-cylinder 4-6-0s in the 5MT power category ('Hall', 'B1', 'N15', 'Black 5'). A Class 5 Pacific would have been an unknown quantity and was considered to be too much of a risk.

What was more difficult to understand was the decision to build both Walschaerts and Caprotti valve gear-fitted locomotives as the BR Standard Class 5. The last 20 LMS-built 'Black 5s' (all entered into service during 1948) had been completed with Caprotti valve gear. The Caprotti gear certainly improved maintenance (increasing the time between piston and valve examinations from 30,000 miles [48,279km] to over 40,000 miles [64,372km]). But the locomotives had a reputation for sluggish performance when starting and at lower speeds also when climbing hills although acknowledged as fast runners on the flat. The issue of poor starting and indifferent slow-speed running was taken up by the UK suppliers of Caprotti valve gear (Associated Locomotive Equipment) and by 1950 they had developed revised valve events. However, by 1950, H. G. Ivatt (the former LMS Chief Mechanical Engineer) no longer had the final say on locomotive matters and decisions on new locomotives required the approval of Riddles and British Railways. Riddles however was a

Left: The revised tender arrangements on later-built Standard Class 5s resulted in detail changes as illustrated on No 73129 (fitted with a BR1B tender). The extended cab floor has a fall plate mounted on the tender. The tender now has a vertical handrail; the second cab handrail has been removed. The cab doors are mounted on the tender. The AWS equipment battery box is mounted under the cab. The cab-side lining is inset from the edge of the cab. *Author's collection*

Above: No 73059 with the AWS pipe clipped to the outside of the footplate valance rather than inside. This method of fixing was observed on a small number of Scottish-based locomotives (including Nos 73077 and 73078 (1960) and also No 73105 (1966). The locomotive is also fitted with a tall vacuum pipe which allowed the fitting of a snowplough. The mounting brackets can be seen below the buffer beam. The numerals on the cab side are the larger 10in (25.4cm) which the Scottish works used. *Author's collection*

believer in the Caprotti concept and was keen to have a small-scale trial of the revised valve gear before applying them to any of the proposed Standard class locomotives. He gave his approval for the final two 'Black 5s' to have the revised valve gear. These two locomotives, Nos 44686 and 44687 (which were placed into traffic in April and May 1951) were quite different from the previous 20 Caprotti examples as the drive to the poppet valves was on the outside, making access and maintenance much easier. The two locomotives also incorporated a high-positioned running plate again to improve access. This running plate was secured to the boiler (not the frames), a design practice that was followed on most of the BR Standard classes.

The revised valve gear was considered a success and footplate crews considered that starting and slow-speed hill climbing were improved without losing any of the Caprotti free-running performance. When one of the earlier batch of 20 Caprotti 'Black 5s' was tested at Rugby in 1949 the Caprotti locomotives were deemed to be more powerful when cut off was below 25% and speed faster than 45mph (72kph) hence the need to revise the valve events for the final two locomotives. These last 'Black 5s' were also fitted with roller bearings, in this case Skefco as

part of a comparison with Timken bearings fitted to other LMS Caprotti 'Black 5s'. One feature of these last two locomotives (not carried over to the Standard Class 5) was the fitment of a double chimney. This was considered for the Standard Class 5s but not fitted.

Given the maintenance advantages it was surprising that only 30 out of 167 Standard Class 5s were fitted with this type of poppet valve gear. Particularly as this small number would mirror the fate of other Caprotti 'Black 5s' in that only certain depots would develop expertise in maintaining the locomotives. Also footplate crews would not develop the familiarity required to get the best out of the class. The mileage run and availability of the Caprotti locomotives had been hampered by the need for fitters from Crewe works to visit depots to carry out specialist work on the valve gear.

A proposal was also made for a Standard Class 5 with Caprotti valve gear and a Crosti boiler or with a boiler based on that of the BR Standard Class 4 (to give adequate clearance within the loading gauge). This came to nothing; any desire to use the Crosti boilers was lukewarm at best and owed more to the persistence of Piero Crosti in asking for his design to be considered by British Railways.

Each design in the new 'Standard' range was allocated

A view of a Standard 5 being
built. Note how the running
plate is mounted to the boiler.
The frames and spring hangers
followed the same style as on
later-built LMS 'Black 5s'.
The lubricator is mounted on
a substantial bracket and the
LNER-style slidebar and
crosshead are clearly visible.
Ian Allan Library

Above left: Maid of Astolat in 1962 having just received an overhaul at Eastleigh works. The nameplate background is painted red and the tender axleboxes are painted yellow. The return crank is the original LNER-style fitment but the original 'chime' whistle behind the chimney has been changed to the 'bell' type.
Author's collection

Above: No 73148 at Perth, May 1964, on the Dundee platform. No 73148 was allocated to 65B St Rollox (Glasgow) for the locomotive's entire service life. The power classification above the number is 5MT. *Ray Oakley / Colour-Rail* (SC1183)

Left: The care worn-state of locomotives in the mid-1960s is shown by an unknown example of the class. The use of the Walschaerts valve gear crosshead on the Caprotti locomotives is shown by the hole at the bottom of the crosshead. *Ian Allan Library*

a drawing office to take primary responsibility for the design, but they also had to use components from a standard list. These components were designed at various works so for instance Derby was responsible for the design of the tender, wheels, axles and springs and Doncaster for cylinders, valve gear, etc.

For the Standard Class 5s the main design office was Doncaster with components being designed at Brighton, Derby and Swindon. Whilst it can be considered that the BR Standard Class 5 was essentially an LMS 'Black 5' this would be a considerable over-simplification. Certainly the boiler was based on the last version (type 3A) of the 'Black 5s' built in 1948. Valve gear and motion was the LNER single slidebar arrangement which owed more to a 'B1' than a 'Black 5'. The clack valves were based on the Southern Region type as used on Bulleid Pacifics.

A comparison below details the differences between the other regions' examples of 4-6-0s having 5MT capability.

What is obvious, is how close the basic dimensions are between the classes; the real differences were in the details such as the design of the steam passages and mechanical details. The key features of the Standard Class 5 were as follows:

1. The horn guides for the axleboxes, unlike the 'Britannia' (BR Standard Class 7) were fitted in the conventional manner being flush with the outer side of the frames. On the 'Britannia' they were placed centrally within the the frame sides following the design of the Bulleid Pacific. The spring hangers followed late LMS practice as used on the postwar examples of the 'Black 5'.

2. The entire class were fitted with Timken roller bearings for both the locomotive (on all axles) and tender. This followed the examples of the later ex-LMS 'Black 5' where a number were fitted with varying types of roller bearings (Timken and Skefco both being used, some on the driving axle only) which had demonstrated reduction in maintenance costs and free running characteristics.

3. Thirty locomotives (Nos 73125 to 73154) were fitted with Caprotti valve gear. This was similar to that fitted on the last two 'Black 5' locomotives Nos 44686 and 44687.

4. The cab and running plate were suspended from the boiler (not on the frames) in the same method as on the 'Britannia' class. But unlike the 'Britannia' the cab floor on the Class 5 was extended but not over the front of the tender. A conventional fall plate was fitted to the tender.

5. The driving wheels were 6ft 2in (1.88m) in diameter which compared with the 6ft 0in (1.83m) drivers of the LMS 'Black 5'.

6. The Caprotti examples were fitted with the same crosshead as on Walschaerts valve gear examples, complete with an unused hole below the crosshead. Another example of using standard components.

Much thought went into the design of the cab and cab controls with a full-size mock-up being constructed for assessment by driving staff. One of the major changes was the reversing wheel which was placed at 90° to the conventional position. On the Caprotti locomotives the reversing wheel was fitted in the conventional position.

The boiler on the Standard Class 5 was based on the design of the later long firebox-type boiler on the LMS 'Black 5'. This was the culmination of a design process stretching back to the original 'Black 5' design of 1936 and was recognised as a good and reliable generator of steam.

Following postwar Southern Railway (SR) and LMS practice the firebox was fitted with a rocking grate which enabled the fireman to break up clinker and allow ash to fall into the ashpan whilst the engine was in motion. The ashpan was fitted with bottom doors (following postwar LMS practice) enabling the pan to be emptied by operating an external lever. This made disposal much easier and safer as the yard staff did not need to use fire irons to rake out clinker.

The wheels were of ex-LMS style with a bevelled rim with the balancing weights formed by steel plates

	Cylinders	Driving Wheels	Boiler Pressure	Grate Area	Tractive Effort
BR Standard Class 5	19in (48.26cm) x 28in (71.12cm)	6ft 2in (1.88m)	225psi (15.7 bar)	28.7sq ft (2.67m²)	26,120ft lb
LMS Class 5	18½in (46.99cm) x 28in (71.12cm)	6ft 0in (1.83m)	225psi (15.7 bar)	28.7sq ft (2.67m²)	25,455ft lb
LNER Class B1	20in (50.8cm) x 26in (66cm)	6ft 2in (1.88m)	225psi (15.7 bar)	27.9sq ft (2.6m²)	26,878ft lb
GWR 'Modified Hall'	18½in (46.99cm) x 30in (76.2cm)	6ft 0in (1.83m)	225psi (15.7 bar)	27.07sq ft (2.51m²)	27,275ft lb

Above: The centre driving wheel and motion on No 73050 as preserved. The return crank has the original LNER-style fixing. Note the two bolts going through the return crank. As with most of the BR's Standard class locomotives the front face of the wheel rim is completely flat.
Author's collection

Overleaf: No 73031 at Rugby testing station undergoing static tests. This locomotive was tested on a number of occasions in 1958 and 1959. Sometimes this was to examine cylinder efficiency and at other times steaming capacity.
Ian Allan Library

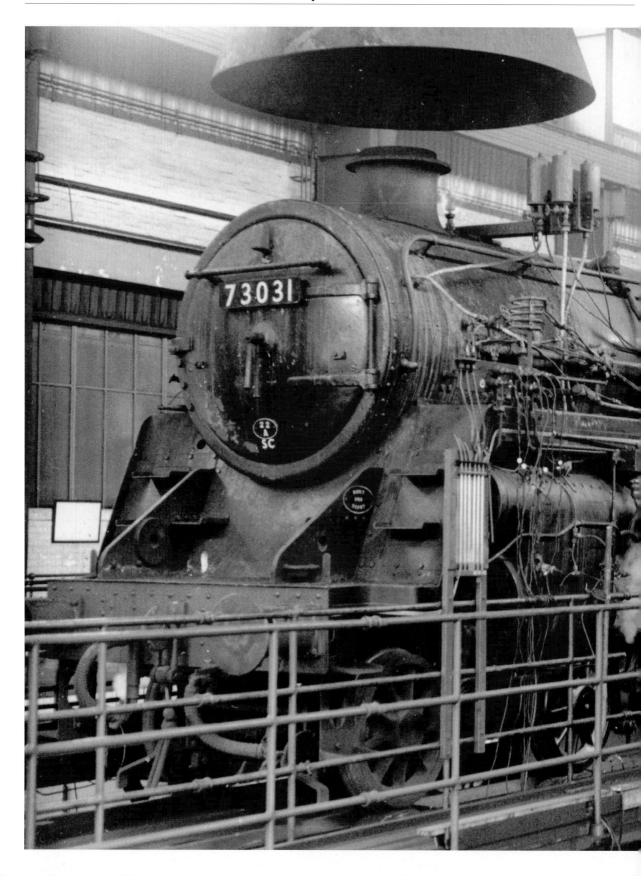

sandwiching the spokes and riveted through from front to back. This followed LMS practice although the diameter at 6ft 2in (1.88m) was the same as on the LNER 'B1'.

A total of five different tenders were fitted to the Standard Class 5, allowing various combinations of coal and water capacity to suit the requirements of the regions to which the locomotives were initially allocated.

The use of Caprotti valve gear required that the mechanical lubricators had to be repositioned as the drive mechanism had to be taken from the rear driving wheels. As a consequence the lubricators were moved closer to the cab (and above the footplate rather than behind the valance). This followed the same arrangements used on the last two Caprotti-fitted LMS 'Black 5' (Nos 44686 and 44687).

An interesting footnote to the class was the use of a modified set of BR Standard 5 frames as the chassis for the gas turbine locomotive GT-3. This locomotive was trialled by BR in the mid-1960s.

Testing

Just after World War Two the Rugby testing plant was finally opened. British Railways took advantage of this and most of the larger standard class locomotives were tested at the plant, including a number of Standard Class 5s.

In 1951 and 1952 locomotive No 73008 was tested

Above: The reversing gear on Caprotti valve geared examples was of a different type to that used on Walschaerts-geared locomotives. The reversing handle is very similar to that fitted to most LMS classes with the handle at 90° to the shaft. On the Walschaerts-geared Standard Class 5s the 'mangle wheel' style of reverser was fitted (similar to the type used on the 'Britannia' class). *Author's collection*

both at the Rugby plant and out on the track between Settle and Carlisle with performance-measuring equipment provided by an ex-LMS Dynamometer car.

No 73030 was tested in 1953 on the rolling road at Rugby. Later, along with No 73031, it was used as part of a trial comparing the efficiency of air-braked wagons with the more traditional vacuum-braked wagons. The trials were run on the Midland main line and were similar to those run with two of the 'Britannia' class (Nos 70043 and 70044).

No 73031 was tested at Rugby in 1958 to examine cylinder efficiency. A further set of tests were run in January 1959 and the subsequent report recommended that a Standard Class 5 locomotive should be built with a Giesel oblong ejector and superheater damper control. However, this was not acted upon. Any modifications and further experiments on steam locomotives were now at an end.

CHAPTER TWO

Construction

The main design office for the class was at Doncaster
with components being designed at Brighton,
Derby and Swindon. All of the class were
built at either Derby or Doncaster.

The class was delivered against 13 different order numbers (the official terminology was Lot Numbers) and all were built at Derby and Doncaster with each batch of locomotives being built for specific regions. This dictated the type of tender to be originally fitted. Some of the boilers and spares were fabricated at Darlington works and then shipped to Derby and Doncaster as required.

The first order (for 30 locomotives) for the Standard Class 5 came in 1952 and was included in the 1953 build programme. By this time over 300 locomotives built to other standard class designs were already in service. Before Derby had made much progress on building this first batch, a further 67 of the class were ordered for building in the 1954 programme.

As each batch was built the opportunity was taken to make some design changes as described below. As building the class took six years to complete, this gave sufficient time for modifications to be designed and implemented. The imperatives to modify were the same as they have always been, but there was a greater readiness by the BR engineers to actually change things for the better.

1. Items that broke or did not work effectively included:
   a. Change of whistle
   b. Changes to the rocking grate
   c. Return crank fixing changed from LNER style to LMS four-bolt fixing
   d. Enlarging the cutaways on valancing (to improve access to lubricators)

   e. Modification of rear of the cab (and the front of tenders)
   f. Modification to the coupling rod section
   g. Modification to the axles for the driving wheel
   h. Blastpipe changes
2. Items that could improve performance or servicing. This included modifications following excessive wear to piston and valves to the lubrication system.

Some parts of the design did not operate as intended and proved troublesome in service. The design team then had to develop modifications. In some cases the modification was to change from, say, an LNER design to that of an earlier LMS design, as in the case of the return crank fixing.

Return crank fixing

The valve gear and motion for all the BR Standard classes was designed at Doncaster. The Standard Class 5s were built with an LNER-style return crank fixing (also used on the 'Britannia' class) but this was subsequently modified to the LMS four-bolt fixing. It would appear that most of the class were subsequently modified to this style of fixing. The change occurred with the first batch of locomotives built at Doncaster (No 73100 built in August 1955) and all subsequent locomotives were built with this style. Following this change, a number of locomotives built with the original LNER crank fixing were changed to

Above: View of the Caprotti drive box and drive shaft. This also shows the LMS four bolt fixing for the crank drive to the Caprotti box. *Author's collection*

Left: The fireman's side of No 73129. *Author's collection*

Number	Works	Date	Tender Type	Return Crank Fixing	Coupling Rods	Whistle	Initial Allocation	Comments
No 73000 to No 73003	Derby	April 1951 to May 1951	BR1	LNER type	Fluted	Behind chimney	LMR	Large holes in driving axles
No 73005 to No 73009	Derby	June 1951 to July 1951	BR1	LNER type	Fluted	Behind chimney	ScR	Large holes in driving axles
No 73010 to No 73029	Derby	August 1951 to January 1952	BR1	LNER type	Fluted	Behind chimney	LMR	Large holes in driving axles
No 73030 to No 73039	Derby	June 1953 to September 1953	BR1	LNER type	Fluted	Behind chimney	ScR	Speedometer fitted Large holes in driving wheels eliminated.
No 73040 to No 73049	Derby	October 1953 to December 1953	BR1	LNER type	Fluted	Behind chimney	LMR	Speedometer fitted
No 73050 to No 73052	Derby	April 1954 to May 1954	BR1G	LNER type	Plain	Behind chimney	SR	Speedometer fitted Changes to rear cab handrails
No 73053 to No 73054	Derby	June 1954	BR1H	LNER type	Plain	Behind chimney	LMR	Speedometer fitted
No 73055 to No 73064	Derby	June 1954 to October 1954	BR1C	LNER type	Plain	Behind chimney	ScR	Speedometer fitted
No 73065 to No 73074	Derby	October 1954 to December 1954	BR1C	LNER type	Plain	Behind chimney	LMR	Speedometer fitted
No 73075 to No 73079	Derby	April 1955 to May 1955	BR1C	LNER type	Plain	Behind chimney	ScR	Speedometer fitted
No 73080 to No 73089	Derby	May 1955 to September 1955	BR1B	LNER type	Plain	Behind chimney	SR	Speedometer fitted
No 73090 to No 73099	Derby	October 1955 to December 1955	BR1C	LNER type	Plain	On top of firebox	LMR	Speedometer fitted
No 73100 to No 73109	Doncaster	August 1955 to January 1956	BR1B	LMS four-bolt type	Plain	On top of firebox	ScR	Speedometer fitted
No 73110 to No 73119	Doncaster	October 1955 to December 1955	BR1F	LMS four-bolt type	Plain	On top of firebox	SR	Speedometer fitted
No 73120 to No 73124	Doncaster	January 1956 to February 1956	BR1B	LMS four-bolt type	Plain	On top of firebox	ScR	Speedometer fitted
No 73125 to No 73134	Derby	July 1956 to October 1956	BR1B	LMS four-bolt type	Plain	On top of firebox	WR	Caprotti valve gear Speedometer fitted
No 73135 to No 73144	Derby	October 1956 to December 1956	BR1C	LMS four-bolt type	Plain	On top of firebox	LMR	Caprotti valve gear Speedometer fitted
No 73145 to No 73154	Derby	January 1957 to June 1957	BR1B	LMS four-bolt type	Plain	On top of firebox	ScR	Speedometer fitted
No 73155 to No 73159	Doncaster	December 1956 to January 1957	BR1B	LMS four-bolt type	Plain	On top of firebox	ER	Speedometer fitted
No 73160 to No 73171	Doncaster	January 1957 to May 1957	BR1B	LMS four-bolt type	Plain	On top of firebox	NER	Speedometer fitted

the four-bolt type of fitting. Certainly a number of condemned locomotives still had the original-style fixing. From photographic evidence I have determined the following locomotives were modified from the LNER type to the four-bolt type:

Nos 73000, 73001, 73007, 73009 (1960), 73014, 73023, 73024, 73036 (1964). Also Nos 73066 (1965), 73090, 73091 and 73094.

Some of the class fitted with the LNER-style crank fixing had this until withdrawal and again from photographic evidence the following are (with date of sighting) locomotives that retained the LNER fitting: Nos 73003 (1966), 73017 (1960), 73022 (1966) and No 73029 (1967). Also Nos 73035 (1967), 73040 (1968), 73056 (1964) and 73071 (1964).

Modification to cab rear

When first built, the cabs had two vertical handrails (similar to those on the 'Britannia' class) mounted either side of the cab entrance. But from No 73050 the tenders were modified and the rear handrail on the cab was removed and a small handrail fitted on the tender. This corresponded with the use of the BR1B and C tenders to which the cab doors were now attached. Also incorporated was a small fall plate over the extended cab floor to reduce draughts on the footplate, something that crews had

Above: No 73040 next to a LMS 'Black 5' at Bolton shed in 1966. This shows the differences in footplates between the LMS Class 5 and the BR version. *Author's collection*

Right: The Walschaerts valve geared locomotives had the BR-style reversing wheel (nicknamed 'mangles' by the footplate staff). The wheel was positioned at 90° to the reversing shaft. Caprotti-fitted locomotives had a more conventional reversing system (see page 22). *Author's collection*

complained about.

Modification to coupling rod sections

Originally the class had lightweight fluted rods, similar to that used on the 'Britannia' class, but following problems with the 'Britannia' many of the standard classes had the rods changed to a heavier plain section and these were fitted from new to No 73050 onwards. However, unlike the 'Britannia' class, the earlier Standard Class 5s did not receive rods to the new design and I have not found any evidence to date that any were subsequently fitted.

Modification to driving wheel axles

The first Standard Class 5 locomotives (as with the 'Britannias' Nos 70000 to 70024) were built with a large hole (approx 2in [5cm] in diameter) bored through the

Above left: The coupling rods, valve gear, brake shoes and sanding gear on No 73096. The wheels followed Stanier LMS practice with bevelled rims. *Author's collection*

Left: A view of the cylinder and valve gear on No 73096 shows the slidebars and crosshead which follow LNER practice. The front face of the lubricator can be seen with a cut-out in the valance. When originally built, the valance covered the face of the lubricator. The orange lining on the footplate edge is done in the Eastleigh style with a line at the top and bottom of the valance. *Author's collection*

Above: An official view of No 73125 when four months old in November 1956. The locomotive, the first of the Caprottis, was first allocated (along with nine others) to Shrewsbury, and then to Patricroft. The lining at the edge of the footplate is a little higher to clear the top of the cam box cover which required part of the valance to be cut away. The locomotive is fitted for Western Region allocation with the WR-style lamp brackets. ATC equipment is fitted, with battery box under the cab. Note the fitment on top of the ejector mounted on the side of the smokebox. The axlebox covers on the tender are in black. *Ian Allan Library*

length of the axle. From photographic evidence this was confined to Nos 73000 to 73029. Subsequently the axles were modified in the same way as on the 'Britannia' class with a solid axle and only a turning centre visible. The 'Britannias' had been modified when on some examples the wheels had moved on the axle. The hollow axle was then replaced with a solid one and all subsequent locomotive batches built with the solid axle. Presumably this was done on the Standard Class 5 as a precautionary measure, although there are no recorded problems with the axles. The hole through the axle had been extensively used on Stanier-designed locomotives (including the 'Duchess' class) without problems but a different method of pressing the wheels onto the axles was used.

Lubricator access

As built, the front face of the lubricator was partially covered by the footplate valance but part of this was

subsequently removed (along the same lines as the 'Britannia') to improve access. The alteration appears to have been made from No 73006 onwards with all locomotives built prior to this retrospectively modified

Lamp irons

As built, for all except the Western Region (WR), the class was fitted with standard lamp irons. Locomotives built for the WR carried the traditional GWR-style lamp irons which were fitted side-on at 90°. However, not all the WR-allocated examples were fitted with the GWR-style lamp irons. For example many of the class allocated to Shrewsbury retained the standard bracket even after repainting in BR dark green livery (examples include Nos 73090, 73091, 73092, 73094 and No 73095). The issue here is whether the locomotives were built for the WR, rather than reallocated. The batch of Caprotti locomotives built for the WR and allocated to Shrewsbury

Above: The crosshead on the Caprottis was the same as that on Walschaerts-fitted locomotives complete with the hole for the drop link which was not required on Caprotti valve gear. *Author's collection*

Right: The battery box for the AWS mounted under the cab for easy access. *Author's collection*

Above: No 73050 displays the original LNER-style return crank fixing. This was changed to the LMS-style four-bolt fixing from 73100. Many (but not all) locomotives fitted with the LNER fixing were modified to the LMS type.
Author's collection

Left: No 73096 shows the revised return crank fixing following LMS practice. The valve gear was designed at Doncaster and followed LNER practice.
Author's collection

from new were all fitted with the GWR-style lamp brackets (Nos 73126, 73127, 73132 and No 73134). When these locomotives at Shrewsbury were transferred to Patricroft in September 1958 and replaced by Walschaerts examples from Patricroft (Nos 73090 to 73098) the replacements arrived with standard lamp brackets which were retained. The GWR-style lamp brackets fitted to Caprottis (Nos 73125 to 73134) were changed once the locomotives were allocated back to Patricroft.

The locomotives transferred to the Southern Region (SR) were all fitted with two additional brackets on the smokebox door (either side of the smokebox dart) to allow the use of the SR-type white route indicator discs. These included Nos 73041, 73080, 73081, 73082, 73083, 73087, 73111, 730113 and 73169. Locomotives allocated to Weymouth were fitted with both GWR- and SR-style lamp brackets.

From 1963 the top lamp bracket was lowered (this was for safety reasons due to the close proximity to overhead power lines) to the right of the smokebox door handle. The corresponding lower lamp iron on the buffer beam was moved to the right. The relocation of the top lamp bracket was a random affair with many locomotives retaining the original fitment. The reality was that only the LMR locomotives actually needed the modification and many of the SR-based examples did not have the bracket lowered. Locomotives known to have been modified include Nos 73001 (1965); 73013, 73025, 73035, 73036 and 73039 (1967); Nos 73059, 73090, 73094, 73100, 73125 and 73126 (1965); Nos 73131, 73141 (1967); and No 73156 (1966), but there were certainly many more, including the undated view of No 73040 illustrated here.

Footplate front steps

The locomotives built at Derby had the top steps fitted on the sloping front platform below the level of the top of the frames, but those built at Doncaster had the steps mounted slightly higher.

Following works repairs, some locomotives ended up with one step at one height and the other at a different height. Examples noted include No 73075 (1964).

Transom tablet catching apparatus

Two locomotives, Nos 73030 and 73031, were for a short period fitted with Transom Tablet catching apparatus. However, nothing else is known to the author of this experiment.

Smowplough fitment and modified front vacuum pipe

A number of the Scottish-based examples were fitted with medium-size snowploughs and this required the front

vacuum pipe to be raised above the buffer beam. The standard vacuum pipe hung below the beam and would therefore be damaged by deep snow when a plough was attached. The snowplough was a standard fitment on these locomotives; the required brackets and attachment points can be located by the raised front vacuum pipe. Photographs of these locomotives with the snowploughs

fitted are rare, but the brackets for attaching the ploughs are usually visible. Examples of locomotives with a tall vacuum pipe and snowplough brackets include Nos 73005, 73006, 73007, 73009, 73055 (1956) and 73056 (1964); Nos 73057, 73058, 73059, 73060, 73061, 73062 and 73063 (1962); also No 73078 (1964).

There were a small number of locomotives observed

Above: No 73040 at Bolton has many of the small modifications made to the class for the last few years in traffic. The front smokebox numberplate is a wood replacement and the smokebox top lamp bracket has been lowered. The shed code has been painted on the lower smokebox. The shed name has been painted on the buffer beam indicating the last overhaul had been at Cowlairs in Glasgow. *Ian Allan Library*

Above: The cab roof of No 73155 shows four bolt heads in the middle of the roof, the purpose of which is not known to the author. The same was seen on a small number of the class. *Ian Allan Library*

with the tall vacuum pipe but without snowplough mounting brackets. It is assumed in these cases that the brackets had been removed with the snowplough. Examples include Nos 73007, 73008 and 73009.

Lifting rings on cab roof

A small number of locomotives were observed with small lifting eyes on the cab roof. These include Nos 73018, 73019, 73020, 73022, 73029 and 73080, also Nos 73082, 73087, 73089, 73113, 73116 and 73117. These do not appear to have been fitted from new and it is presumed that this was carried out at a specific works, possibly Eastleigh, as all of the locomotives listed were allocated to the SR. No other evidence has been found to confirm this (the RCTS notes on the class confirm the Eastleigh theory).

Cab roof bolts

From photographs a small number of the class were observed with a cluster of prominent bolts on the cab roof. Examples include Nos 73090, 73091, 73092, 73096, 73155 and 73171. It is not known to the author why these were fitted.

Speedometer fitment

From No 73030 onwards all Standard Class 5 locomotives were fitted from new with the Smith-Stone speed indicator.

Some locomotives were built without this equipment but were subsequently fitted, these include Nos 73007, 73014, 73018 and 73029. The official records used in the RCTS notes on the class also list in addition Nos 73010, 73011 and 73022 but I have not been able to confirm this with photographic evidence.

ATC and AWS equipment

When built, the class was not fitted with the BR Automatic Warning System (AWS) but those allocated to the WR were fitted with Automatic Train Control (ATC). This was fitted at Swindon following delivery of the first Standard Class 5 locomotives from Derby and Doncaster works.

The ATC equipment could be identified by the following:

1. Battery box under the cab on the driver's side (left-hand side looking from the front). The box was mounted at 90^0 to the frames.
2. Pipe (conduit) along the whole length of the running plate, either under the valance or more visibly on the bottom edge (sometimes passing under the lubricator). Examples with the conduit visible include Nos 73026, 73034 and 73036.
3. Box-shaped contact shoe bolted to the front of the bogie.
4. A circular fitting on the top of the exhaust ejector (the ejector is located at the rear edge of the smokebox on the driver's side).

Examples of locomotives fitted with ATC include Nos 73023, 73025, 73026, 73034, 73035 and 73036. The Caprotti examples sent from new to Shrewsbury (Nos 73125 to 73134) were also fitted with ATC. Again locomotives moved to the WR from other regions did not

Above: No 73054 on the Lickey bank south of Birmingham. The locomotive is painted in BR green livery with a Western Region red spot route indicator. *Author's collection*

necessarily have ATC fitted, examples including the batch Nos 73090 to 73098 sent to Shrewsbury from Patricroft in 1958. The RCTS list the following additional (to those listed above) locomotives to have been fitted with ATC. These were Nos 73012, 73013, 73014, 73015, 73017, 73018, 73019, 73020, 73021, 73022, 73024, 73027, 73028 and 73029.

In line with most of the modern steam locomotives in traffic during BR days a decision was made to fit a standard design of an automatic warning system (AWS), but as with many other classes the fitment was a haphazard affair and significant number of the Standard Class 5 were never fitted with the equipment.

The system was similar to the ATC used on the WR but could be identified by:

1. Revised battery position under the cab, the larger, flat face of the battery facing outwards. The cover had reinforcing ribbing.
2. A 'bash' plate below the front buffer beam. Sometimes the brackets to attach this plate were on the front face of the buffer beam and occasionally behind.
3. The conduit connecting the shoe from the bogie to the cab was hidden behind the valance. However, a number

of locomotives had the conduit on the outside, examples (with date of sighting) being Nos 73059, 73077, 73078 (1960) and 73105 (1966).

4. A small circular contact shoe under the leading pony truck.

Locomotives from No 73162 appear to have been fitted with AWS from new. From scrutinising photographs of Standard Class 5s a number were fitted with AWS as follows:

Nos 73007, 73009, 73030, 73033, 73035, 73039, 73041, 73040 and 73043. Also Nos 73056, 73060, 73062, 73063, 73067, 73070 and 73078. Nos 73080, 73081, 73082, 73083, 73085. 73086, 73089 and 73098. Also Nos 73100, 73105, 73107, 73112, 73113, 73114, 73115, 73116 and 73118. Nos 73125, 73134, 73144, 73153, 73163, 73169 and No 73171.

A small number of AWS-fitted locomotives were observed without the 'bash' plate below the buffer beam. Examples includes Nos 73089 and 73168, but it is not known to the author why this was the case, possibly due to accident damage.

Whistle location

When first built, the class were fitted with a 'chime'-type whistle located behind the chimney and operated by a cable running down the handrail. On occasions the whistle would stick open. Subsequently locomotives from No 73090 were built with the whistle mounted on top of the

Above: No 73006 at Cowlairs works in 1959. The Manson tablet catcher for use on the Highland lines is mounted on the side of the cab. *Author's collection*

Right: No 73036 allocated to Shrewsbury shed departs from Trench Crossing on the line between Stafford and Wellington with a Stafford–Shrewsbury train in the early 1960s. Locomotives from Shrewsbury were regular performers on these light stopping trains. The author travelled from this station many times behind a Standard Class 5. No 73036 is fitted with ATC equipment, a standard WR fitment. Note that the top lamp bracket has been lowered. *Ian Allan Library*

firebox. The RCTS list the change to firebox-mounted whistles from locomotive No 73100, but analysis of photographs indicates that No 73090 onwards did not have the whistle behind the chimney. Many of the original 'chime' whistles were replaced by a 'bell'-type whistle which was mounted in the same position behind the chimney.

Driver's name clips on cab

A small number of Western Region locomotives had a small bracket fitted to the cab side which allowed the driver's name to be displayed. Examples include No 73003, and the RCTS notes also list Nos 73065 and 73138. The brackets were also fitted to the 'Britannias' but like those on the Class 5, never seem to have been used. I have not found a photograph showing one in use for either class.

Tablet catcher

Locomotives working on the Somerset & Dorset line were fitted with the Whitaker tablet system. This equipment was fitted to the driver's side at the front of the tender on the outside, examples included Nos 73087 and 73116. The RCTS notes also list Nos 73001, 73019, 73028, 73047, 73049, 73050, 73052, 73054 and 73068. For locomotives loaned from other SR depots to the Somerset & Dorset line for summer services the tablet equipment would in general be removed when the locomotive was returned to depot.

Locomotives regularly working on the Highland main line were fitted with the Manson-type tablet catcher. The equipment was mounted on the driver's side of the cab. In the case of the Scottish Region locomotives it was mounted on the lower half of the cab side sheet. Examples fitted include Nos 73006, 73008 and 73009.

CHAPTER THREE

Tenders

Each of the receiving regions requested
a tender of a specific type in an attempt to match
with proposed workings. A total of six different
types were fitted behind the Standard Class 5.

The tender for the Standard Class 5 was a combination of new designs and tenders already existing within the range of standard types. All the standard tenders shared the same wheels, underframe and wheelbase and all were fitted with roller bearings.

Each of the receiving regions requested a tender of a specific type in an attempt to match with proposed workings. For instance the WR specified the BR1G tender, the LMR the BR1C whilst the SR requested the BR1F. From a range of standard tenders a total of six different types were fitted behind the Standard Class 5 locomotives as listed below.

The basic BR standard tender was the BR1 with narrow coal bunker, introduced in 1951 for the 'Britannia'

class. This had a 4,250gal (19,320.5-litre) water capacity and a load of 7 tons (7,427.4kg) of coal. However, it soon became clear that the water capacity was marginal and led to the development of the BR1A tender modified to carry 5,000gal (22,730-litre) of water and 7 tons (7,427.4kg) of coal. The distinguishing feature is a much taller dome at the rear of the coal space. The BR1A tender was intended to be fitted behind the first of the Standard Class 5s, but before this happened the tender design was modified to allow the fitment of a conventional fall plate on the tender to cover the gap in the extended cab floor. This revised tender was designated BR1G and except for the changes for the fall plate it was identical to the BR1A.

The tenders were as follows:

Type	BR1	BR1B	BR1C	BR1F	BR1G	BR1H
Coal – tons	7	7	9	7	7	7
kg	7,427.4	7,427.4	9,144.5	7,427.4	7,427.4	7,427.4
Water – gallons	4,250	4,725	4,725	5,625	5,000	4,250
litres	19,320.5	21,480	21,480	25,571	22,730	19,320.5
Weight – tons	49.15	51.25	53.25	55.25	52.50	49.15
kg	49,939	52,073	554,105	56,137	53,343	49,939
Axle load – tons	16.8	17.1	17.75	18.5	18.5	16.8
kg (max)	17,069.8	17,374.6	18,035	18,797	18,797	17,069.8
Comments	No fall plate fitted	Increased water capacity. Fall plate and gangway doors fitted	Fall plate and gangway doors fitted	Not fitted with water pick-up apparatus	Identical to BR1A but fitted with fall plate and gangway doors	

The extended cab floor and fall plate are clearly visible. The tender is a BR1B with the handrail on the tender. *Author's collection*

Above: No 73115 with the tender changed from the original BR1F to that of a BR1B. Only a small number of Standard 5s were recorded as having tenders changed from that originally fitted. *(RP)*

BR1. Originally fitted to Nos 73000 to 730049.

BR1B. These were fitted to the majority of the class Nos 73080 to 73089, Nos 73100 to 73109, Nos 73120 to 73124, Nos 73125 to 73134 and Nos 73145 to 73171. All had 7 ton (7,427.4kg) coal and 4,250gal (19,320.5-litre) water capacity. They had a Stanier-like appearance being very similar in appearance to the last tenders built by the LMS for the 'Black 5' and the final two 'Coronation' class locomotives.

BR1C. Fitted to Nos 73065 to 73079, Nos 73090 to 73099 and Nos 73135 to 73144. These were superficially identical to the BR1B, the only difference being coal capacity; the 1C carried 9 tons (9,144.5kg) and the 1B 7 tons (7,427.4kg). Both looked identical except for the addition of a coal space partition plate on the 1B to reduce coal capacity.

BR1F. This was the type preferred by the Eastern Region when fitted to '9F' locomotives. It had 7 tons (7,427.4kg) coal capacity but carried 5,625gal (25,571-litres) of water. On the Standard Class 5 locomotives (Nos 73110 to 73119) which were sent to the SR (the region did not have water troughs) the increased water capacity would be of benefit. The water capacity proved invaluable when an

SR-based locomotive worked all the way to Sheffield without taking on water. The BR1F tenders were not fitted with water pick-up apparatus.

BR1G. Identical to BR1A but fitted with a fall plate and gangway doors. these tenders were originally fitted to Nos 73050, 73051 and 73052. The BR1G was the preferred tender for locomotives allocated to the Western Region.

BR1H. Fitted to Nos 73053 to 73064. These were identical to the BR1 tender but with a small fall plate and gangway doors.

Rear steps on top of tender
On the 'Britannia' class the first batch of BR1 tenders (fitted to Nos 70000 to 70024) did not have a step adjacent to the water filer on the top rear of the tender. This was considered a safety issue so subsequent tenders were built with a step and earlier tenders modified. A similar problem

Above: No 73134 is seen at Patricroft shed in 1968. The tender is a BR1B in plain black and the cab-side numbers are the larger 10in (25.4cm). *Author's collection*

type was signified by a red stripe across the yellow cover. Locomotives noted with plain yellow axlebox covers include Nos 73019, 73071 (1964) and 73097 (1964). Also Nos 73116, 73130 (1964) and 73132 (1964).

Tender exchanges

As with many other locomotive classes in the dying days of steam, depots would make tender exchanges to keep locomotives in traffic and the Standard Class 5 was no exception. However, only a small number have been clearly identified.

occurred with BR1, BR1G-type tenders for the Standard Class 5. These were built without a step but all were subsequently modified.

Axlebox covers

When delivered the roller-bearing axlebox covers were painted black, but with subsequent changes to the type of oil used all were painted yellow. A further change of oil

Number	Date Observed	Original Tender	Changed Tender	Comment
No 73005	1964	BR1	BR1	Seen with a green tender from a withdrawn 'Clan' class locomotive.
No 73082	1966	BR1B	BR1F	
No 73085	1965	BR1B	BR1F	
No 73110	1966	BR1F	BR1B	
No 73111	1965	BR1F	BR1B	Tenders swapped between Nos 73085 and 73111
No 73115	1965	BR1F	BR1B	Tender from No 75075

The BR1B tender as
fitted to the Caprotti-
fitted locomotives.
Author's collection

Above left: The BR1 tender as first built without a step on the top rear of the tender. The step that was subsequently added is clearly visible.

Above: The modified tender also has yellow axlebox covers and is carrying overhead warning flashes. *Ian Allan Library*

Left: Some SR allocated locomotives were fitted with a BR1F tender which had additional water capacity. This was important on the SR as it did not have water troughs. The elegant lines of the BR1F tender are evident fitted to No 73113 *Lyonnesse. Ian Allan Library*

Above: A rear view of a BR1B tender. *Author's collection*

Above: A rear view of a BR1G tender. *Author's collection*

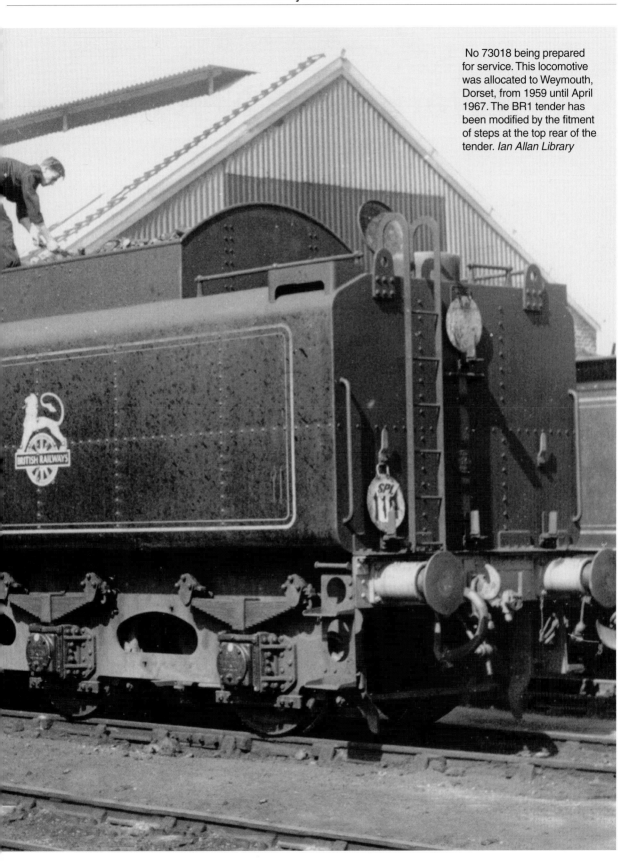

No 73018 being prepared for service. This locomotive was allocated to Weymouth, Dorset, from 1959 until April 1967. The BR1 tender has been modified by the fitment of steps at the top rear of the tender. *Ian Allan Library*

CHAPTER FOUR

Liveries and Names

The livery adopted by BR for mixed traffic
locomotives and used on the Standard Class 5
was gloss black with grey, cream and red lining
on the running plate, cab and tender sides.

The liveries applied to the Standard Class 5 locomotives were as follows:

BR mixed trafic black

The livery adopted by BR for mixed traffic locomotives and used on the Standard Class 5 was gloss black with grey, cream and red lining on the running plate, cab and tender sides. This was essentially the old-style LNWR passenger livery, Riddles having started his railway career with the LNWR. In this livery the bottom edge of the running plate valance had a grey line with the inside edge having a thinner cream line, then a gap before a single red line parallel with the grey line. The cab side was lined out in a similar fashion with two red lines on each boiler band. The cylinders were also finished with two pairs of red lining (a pair at each end).

When first completed, No 73000 was test run painted in grey undercoat before being finished in black mixed traffic livery (but with different lining on the valance). No 73000 was displayed at Marylebone Station, London on 26 April 1951. The change in the livery incorporated two red lines on the footplate valance, one at the top and one at the bottom (instead of the grey/cream/red combination) and followed the style of the orange line forming a panel on the 'Britannia' class. This was subsequently changed to a grey/cream line near the bottom edge with a red line inside. No 73000 received this alteration by 10 May 1952 when the locomotive was photographed.

For Caprotti locomotives the lining on the cylinders was usually omitted, although the preserved example has lined out cylinders. On some of the Caprotti locomotives overhauled at Crewe the lining on the valance was slightly higher up to avoid the cut-out allowed for the cylinder cam box cover. On others the lining was on the bottom edge of the valance with a short break in the lining where the cutout was. An example of this was No 73145.

The lining on cab sides varied, with some having the lining close to the edge of the cab (common on Doncaster overhauls) and others with the lining much further in from the edge of the cab. Locomotives with this style of lining also had small variations in the size and location of the lining on the tender.

Above right: The lining on the footplate valance is ruled to clear the cutaway in the valance to clear the top of the Caprotti cam boxes. *Author's collection*

Right: The Eastleigh version of BR green livery with the use of an orange line at both the top and bottom of the valance. A vertical line at the end of the valance formed an elongated panel. When Swindon originally painted locomotives green a single orange line at the bottom of the valance was used. Eastleigh works followed the same style of lining as on the rebuilt Bulleid Pacifics when lining out Standard Class 5 locomotives. *Author's collection*

When these locomotives were moved to other regions and were overhauled at Doncaster, Eastleigh, Darlington and Cowlairs the green lined livery was retained. What is not clear is if all these works actually repainted the locomotives in green or just touched up the paintwork. When Eastleigh became responsible for overhauls on the class they introduced another lining variant, in that the lining on the cab side formed a rectangular panel (similar to the way rebuilt Bulleid pacifics were lined out) instead of the single orange line at the bottom edge of the valance applied by Swindon. Examples of this style include Nos 73029 and 73054 (1964).

When Darlington applied the green livery, some locomotives had the orange line further from the bottom edge than the Swindon style. The list of lined green locomotives is as follows:

Nos 73001, 73003, 73012, 73014, 73015, 73018, 73021, 73023, 73024, 73026, 73027 and 73029. Also Nos 73031, 73034, 73035, 73036, 73054, 73068, 73090, 73091, 73092, 73094, 73095, 73096 and 73097. Lined green livery lasted until the end of steam, with No 73035 still in this livery in 1968.

Some locomotives overhauled at Doncaster and Eastleigh were repainted but the valance was not lined. Examples include No 73003 (in dark green), 73132 (Darlington, 1964) and 73145 (1962).

BR green

The locomotives allocated to the Western Region were delivered in BR lined black livery but many were subsequently repainted in fully lined BR dark green passenger livery. This was applied to the class on the region from the end of 1958 (Nos 73001 and 73068) during overhauls usually at Swindon although Wolverhampton also applied BR dark green livery to Nos 73037, 73093 and 73097.

The livery was the same as applied to all BR passenger locomotives with orange and black lining to the cab sides and tender sides, with the boiler bands and cylinders lined in orange. The finish on Standard Class 5s differed from that on the 'Britannia' class in that the lining on the valance was made up of a single orange line at the bottom (rather than at the top and bottom).

Unlined black and green

In early 1964 the use of lining on all steam locomotives (both black and green) was supposed to have been stopped and the locomotives outshopped in plain black or green. Darlington, Eastleigh and Cowlairs certainly continued to line out Standard Class 5s. It is known that Inverurie works was still lining out 'Black 5s' as late as March 1965 (Nos 44998, 45214, 45483 and 45489).

Crewe appear to have been the only works to have adhered to the edict to stop lining out. As mentioned in *Locomotives in Detail: No 5 Riddles Class 6/7 Standard Pacifics* the plain BR green appeared a different shade to the lined out version of standard BR dark green, being more like a darker khaki (army) green. This looked drab even when clean. The only known examples of complete unlined liveries included No 73069 which was observed in unlined black when outshopped from Crewe in September 1966. Other locomotives including No 73134 (1968) were observed with lining on the locomotive but none on the tender.

Only a small number of Standard Class 5s were changed back to BR dark green livery once repainted black. One example, No 73037, was repainted from lined green back to black in February 1964.

Large cab side numbers

Those locomotives being overhauled and repainted at Darlington, Cowlairs and St Rollox received larger cab side numerals (10in [25cm] instead of the normal 8in [20cm]). The application of 10in (25cm) was inconsistent at Darlington with some locomotives having 8in (20cm) numerals applied. Examples include Nos 73008, 73009 (1962) and 73056, (1964), 73057, 73059, 73060, 73075,

Above left: No 73094 at Birmingham New Street, August 1962. The locomotive is in lined green livery with a large BR totem on the tender. At this date No 73094 was allocated to Gloucester (Barnwood) and would have been a regular visitor to Birmingham. *Author's collection*

73107, 73108, 73110, 73111, 73112, 73113, 73117, 73118, 73121, 73134 and 73154.

Eastleigh works also used larger cab side numerals on some (but not all) of the class overhauled there in the early 1960s.

Power classification

The power classification 'branding' for the cab side (above the number) of the class was variable, with just about every possible variant being used. Derby and Horwich: 5, Doncaster: BR 5, Cowlairs: 5MT Eastleigh managed a number of variants including 5p 5f, 5P 5F, 5P/5F (Nos 73082 to 73087).

There were some examples where no classification 'branding' appears to have been applied. Examples include Nos 73049 (1956), 73092, 73117 (1955).

Above: No 73158 at York in August 1957. The locomotive is finished in BR black with the first style of BR totem on the tender. At this time the locomotive was one of two allocated to Kings Cross (34A), before being moved on to Cricklewood then Canklow. *Author's collection*

Route availabliity indicator – WR

On the Western Region all locomotives carried a coloured spot below the locomotive number on the cab side (approx 2in [5cm] in diameter) indicating the routes on which the locomotives were allowed to work. On the Standard Class 5s this 'spot' was red. When the locomotives were removed from the WR these route indicators were left on, but would be lost at the next repaint. The application of the red spot varied, as No 73026 (based at Leamington shed) when outshopped in BR dark green from Eastleigh did not have the spot although at this time Leamington had moved to the LM Region. Examples seen with the red spot include Nos 73003, 73021, 73024, 73926, 73027 and 73031 (1960), 73034, 73035, 73036, 73054 and 73068 (1958), also No 73092. Not all green finished locomotives received the spot. Examples include Nos 73091, 73092 and 73094 (1962), 73095, 73096 and 73097 (1964).

Power classification on buffer beams

Locomotives overhauled at Doncaster had 'Cl 5' painted on the firemans side of the front buffer beam. Examples include Nos 73105, 73109 (1960), 73163 (1957) and 73166 (1956). St Rollox also painted in a similar style 'B.R. 5' on the fireman's side of the front buffer beam.

Depot names on buffer beams

When Cowlairs repainted locomotives the depot name was generally painted on the front buffer beam and examples include Nos 73026 (Bolton, 1967), 73040 (Bolton, 1968), No 73057 (Corkerhill, 1964), 73059 (Polmadie, 1965), 73062 (Motherwell, 1956), No 73098 (Polmadie, 1964), 73121 and 73100 (Corkerhill, 1964), 73101 (Corkerhill, 1966), 73125 (Patricroft), 73134 (Patricroft, 1968), 73141 (Patricroft), 73134 (St Rollox), No 73154 (St Rollox, 1965) and 73105 (Grangemouth). However, it appears that Eastleigh applied only one shed name, Leamington Spa, to No 73026 in 1965. No 73156 was also observed with Leamington Spa on the buffer beam but it is not known to the author where this was applied.

Water treatment

The locomotives allocated to the SR had TIA (Traitement Intégral Armand) water treatment equipment fitted. This

was indicated by a yellow spot (for the French system) and later by a yellow triangle when the BR system was fitted. According to some sources the reason for changing from the yellow spot to a triangle was to avoid confusion with the (yellow spot) WR route availability indicator. All the locomotives allocated to the SR were given the water treatment indicator (Nos 73080 to 73089 and Nos 73110 to 73119). When Standard Class 5s from the WR and LMR were allocated to the SR between 1964 and 1965 some appear to have received the yellow triangle symbol. Examples include Nos 73029 (observed in green livery, 1967), 73092 (observed in green livery, 1966) and 73171. It is likely that all locomotives reallocated to the SR received the indicator. Unfortunately in most photographs the locomotives are too dirty to identify the indicator.

Overhead warning

From April 1960, following continental practice, BR began fitting white enamel plates painted with the

Above: No 73141 at Birkenhead, March 1967. A number of livery changes common in the last years of steam are visible, including a hand-painted smokebox numberplate and a lowered top lamp bracket. Note the hand-painted shed code of 9H. A worker has taken the trouble of cleaning the shed name painted on the buffer beam. *Ian Allan Library*

Right: No 73092 in BR green livery leaves Waterloo in June 1966. The triangle under the number indicates that water treatment equipment is fitted. No 73092 had originally been allocated to the Western Region (Shrewsbury and Gloucester), hence the green livery. It was then reallocated to Eastleigh and Guildford, hence the use of water treatment. Note the revised cab handrails with the fitting of the BR1B or BR1C tenders. *Ian Allan Library*

symbolic warning sign of forked lightning (in red) to strategic positions on the boiler cladding. These were to warn of the proximity of overhead power wires. As the use of electrification extended there were a number of

accidents where steam locomotive crews came into contact with the overhead power lines when either trimming coal, filling the tender or fitting lamps. The position of these warning flashes varied from locomotive to locomotive, but the usual placing was as follows:

a. On the sloping front platform.
b. Rear of the tender.
c. On the firebox sides.
d. On the boiler sides.

Yellow tender axlebox covers

When built, the tender axlebox covers were painted black but in common with all BR's standard classes the bearings were of the roller type. However, to indicate to shed staff that the tenders had roller bearings and to differentiate them from plain bearings the covers were subsequently painted yellow. When the roller bearings had the lubrication type changed this was indicated to maintenance staff by painting the axlebox yellow with a red stripe. In reality this appeared to be a random affair. I have colour

photographs clearly showing plain yellow in 1963 and in 1964 (No 73097 at York). Other examples include Nos 73019, 73071 (1964), 73116, 73130 (1964) and 73132 (1964). However, in the majority of cases the colour of the axlebox covers is impossible to determine under the general covering of grime and filth. Even where the locomotive was reasonably clean the axlebox covers always appeared to be liberally covered in an oily grime.

Left: No 73069 at Manchester Victoria, 4 August 1968, before working a special train. The locomotive and tender are in plain BR black livery. Note the axlebox covers on the tender are painted yellow. *Ian Allan Library*

Smokebox number plates

In the last days of steam from 1966 onwards, many locomotives were seen without a smokebox numberplate, including No 73163. Others were fitted with replacement plates made at the depot (usually from wood and with hand-painted numbers). Examples include, No 73000 (seen in October 1965), 73022 (seen in April 1965), 73029 (seen in June 1967), 73066 (1966), 73100 (1966), No 73117 (1966) and 73125 (1968). In some cases the number was chalked in the space once occupied by the smokebox plate. Examples includes Nos 73001 and 73018. Other locomotives had the number painted on the smokebox door, such as No 73092 (1967).

Some Scottish Region locomotives were seen with a white border painted around the smokebox numberplate. Examples include Nos 73007, 73057 and 73075 (1962). Also Nos 73107 and 73121 in around 1964-5.

Many classes of locomotives on the Scottish Region could also be seen with a blue background to name and number plates. The Standard Class 5s were no exception and examples of blue-backed smokebox plates seen includes Nos 73008 (1955) and 73058 (allocated to Polmadie).

Nameplates

As the result of a Southern Region staff suggestion scheme a number of locomotives were between May 1959 and September 1962 given names formerly carried by 'King Arthur' class locomotives as follows:

No 73080 *Merlin* (February 1961)
No 73081 *Excalibur* (February 1961)
No 73082 *Camelot* (August 1959)
No 73083 *Pendragon* (October 1959)
No 73084 *Tintagel* (? 1959)
No 73085 *Melisande* (August 1959)
No 73086 *The Green Knight* (December 1959)
No 73087 *Linette* (May 1961)
No 73088 *Joyous Gard* (May 1961)
No 73089 *Maid of Astolat* (May 1959)
No 73110 *The Red Knight* (May 1959)
No 73111 *King Uther* (January 1960)
No 73112 *Morgan Le Fay* (February 1961)
No 73113 *Lyonnesse* (April 1960)
No 73114 *Etarre* (December 1959)
No 73115 *King Pellinore* (February 1960)
No 73116 *Iseult* (September 1962)

Above: One of the nameplates specifically made for the class and fitted between 1959 and 1962. The majority had a black background but in 1962 *Maid of Astolat* was certainly observed in red. *Ian Allan Library*

No 73117 *Vivien* (April 1961)
No 73118 *King Leodegrance* (February 1960)
No 73119 *Elaine* (June 1959)

Right: No 73043 still in mixed traffic livery in July 1967. Note the power classification '5' above the number. The draught screen fitted between the cab and tender is in the usual ripped and torn state. On the members of the class fitted with the two vertical cab handrails the cab doors were attached to the cab. On locomotives with a single handrail the cab doors were hung from the tender. On the cab roof are the four bolt heads in the middle of the cab roof, seen on some examples based on the SR. *Ian Allan Library*

The dates of naming are when the locomotives were observed leaving Eastleigh works with plates affixed. The process of naming was a leisurely affair as it took nearly three years from the first one to receive a name (No 73119 *Elaine*) to the last example (No 73116 *Iseult*) to be named in September 1962. These nameplates were not simply transferred from the withdrawn locomotives (the plates had 'King Arthur' class under the name) but were cast specifically for the Standard Class 5. Both black and red painted backgrounds to the plates were used. Examples of red backgrounds include No 73089 *Maid of Astolat* (1962) but the majority of nameplates were finished with a black background.

There was a proposal to paint the SR-named locomotives in lined green livery but this was not followed

through and all remained in lined black. As with all named classes the plates were removed in the period 1964 to 1965. As an example, in May 1965 (as reported by the RCTS) the status of some of the class was as follows:

No 73086 *The Green Knight*: Both plates intact
No 73112 *Morgan Le Fay*: Both plates removed (locomotive withdrawn in June 1965)
No 73113 *Lyonnesse*: One plate only
No 73115 *King Pellinore*: One plate only
No 73118 *King Leodegrance*: Both plates removed.
No 73119 *Elaine*: Both plates intact.

No 73050 following preservation has carried the name *City of Peterborough*.

CHAPTER FIVE

Engines in Service

The Standard 5 Class was considered in the same
light as the 'Hall', 'Black 5' and 'B1'. However, on the
SR the class gained an excellent reputation and in
some cases was preferred to a Bulleid Light Pacific.

As the class effectively replaced all the previous pre-nationalisation two-cylinder 4-6-0s ('Black 5', 'Hall', 'B1') any new regional traffic requirement for a '5MT' would be covered by the BR Standard Class 5.

Allocations
As a result all the regions placed orders for the class and therefore they could be seen at most mainline depots throughout Britain, although the North Eastern examples were confined to the Leeds and West Riding areas. It must be remembered that over 180 of 'B1' class 4-6-0s were delivered to the Eastern Region between 1948 and June 1950 so the Eastern and North Eastern Regions already had enough locomotives in this category as well as having a large number of 'V2' mixed traffic locomotives.

On the Southern the class effectively replaced 'S15' and 'N15' locomotives which by the early 1950s were 30 years old. As the 'S15' and 'N15' classes were withdrawn additional Standard Class 5s were allocated. In later years the Standard 5 supplemented Bulleid Pacifics, particularly on the heavy stopping trains between Bournemouth and Waterloo.

Except for the Caprotti examples, no attempt was made to 'block' allocate locomotives to a smaller number of sheds; the Standard 5 Class was considered in the same light as the 'Hall', 'Black 5' and 'B1'. However, on the SR that class gained an excellent reputation and in some cases was preferred to a Bulleid Light Pacific, particularly as it was not prone to slipping.

The 30 Caprotti locomotives built were only ever allocated to a small number of sheds. It was thought that this would make maintenance easier and that fitting staff could become familiar with the idiosyncrasies of the valve gear. A total of 10 (Nos 73125 to 73134) new locomotives went to Shrewsbury in 1956 but were swapped in September 1958 for a similar number of Walschaerts-fitted locomotives with Patricroft (Manchester). Patricroft had a sizeable allocation from that date through to the closure of the shed on 1 July 1968 and one of the last Standard Class 5s, No 73069, was moved to Carnforth. Other LMR sheds to have Caprotti locomotives included Rowsley (district) which had six for working fast freights to Derby, Holyhead and Leicester. On the Scottish Region, Caprotti locomotives were well thought of and used regularly on fast passenger trains to Aberdeen.

Some depots had a long association with the class and had a sizeable allocation, including Patricroft which took delivery of the first example in November 1951 (No 73024) and retained a large allocation up to closure in 1968. Similarly Shrewsbury received the first locomotive in September 1953 (No 73017) and had a sizeable 'stud' until the shed closed in 1966.

The strange allocation of one of the class (No 73071) to King's Cross in 1957 was for testing AWS, which at that time was only on a section of the East Coast main line. No 73071 left King's Cross after a few months.

From the mid-1960s onwards the allocation of Standard Class 5s moved to depots not previously

Above: No 73097 at York, April 1964 in ex-works condition. Note the yellow axlebox covers. The locomotive does not have a WR red spot route indicator. *Author's collection*

Below: No 73040 in March 1968 with the shed name painted on the buffer beam. The smokebox number plate is hand painted and the top lamp bracket has been lowered. *Author's collection*

Standard Class 5s from Shrewsbury were used regularly on the Central Wales line between Swansea and Craven Arms (then on to Shrewsbury). No 73091 is approaching Sugar Loaf tunnel on a northbound train, August 1961.
Ian Allan Library

In the table below the shed codes relate to the specific dates as many depots were renumbered over time and some moved from one region to another, so Annesley was originally 38B (on the Eastern Region) but became 16D (LMR) in 1958 and then 16B (LMR) in 1963.

December 1957	December 1960	January 1963	1965	January 1967
Nottingham (16A) 3			Nuneaton (5E) 7	
Leicester Mid (15C) 9		Woodford (1G, 2F) 6		
	Huddersfield (55G) 4	Huddersfield (55G) 1		
Leeds (Holbeck) (55A) 5	Leeds (Holbeck) (55A) 5			
Sheffield (Millhouses) (19B) 5	Rowsley (17C)	Rowsley (16J) 6		
Derby (17A) 5	Derby (17A) 4			
Holyhead (6J) 5	Holyhead (6J) 3	Llandudno (6G) 3		Bolton (9K) 11
Chester (M) (6A) 5	Chester (M) (6A) 8	Chester (M) (6A) 4	Wrexham (Croes Newydd) (6C) 3	Wrexham (Croes Newydd) (6C) 1
Patricroft (10C) 12	Patricroft (26F) 12	Patricroft (26F, 9H) 11	Patricroft (9H) 26 Stirling (65J) 3	Patricroft (9H) 42
Perth (63A) 6	Perth (63A) 8	Perth (63A) 4	Motherwell (66B) 1	Motherwell (66B) 2
Eastfield (65A) 7	Eastfield (65A) 5	Eastfield (65A) 4	Eastfield (65A) 3	Carstairs (66E) 1
Corkerhill (67A) 10	Corkerhill (67A) 10	Corkerhill (67A) 15	Corkerhill (67A) 15	Corkerhill (67A) 5
Polmadie (66A) 12	Polmadie (66A) 15	Polmadie (66A) 15 St Rollox (65B) 10	Polmadie (66A) 11 St Rollox (65B) 8 Aberdeen (Ferryhill) (61B) 2	Polmadie (66A) 6
Shrewsbury (84G) 10	Shrewsbury (84G) 16	Shrewsbury (84G, 6D) 10	Shrewsbury (6D) 7	
Cardiff Canton (86C) 4		Gloucester (Barnwood) (85C) 9	Gloucester Horton Rd (85B) 1	
Bristol St Philip's Marsh (82B) 5				
Oxley (84B) 3		Oxley (84B, 2B) 1	Oxley (2B) 14	
Tyseley (84E) 2	Tyseley (84E) 6		Tyseley (2A) 4	
Swindon (82C) 7	Swindon (82C) 3	Swindon (82C) 4		
Chester (WR) 84K 4			Oxford (81F) 10	
Bath Green Park (71G) 5	Bath Green Park (71G) 8	Bath Green Park (71G) 2	Bath Green Park (82F) 6	
Stewarts Lane (73A) 9			Feltham (70B) 2	
Eastleigh (71A) 2		Eastleigh (71A) 1	Eastleigh (70D) 14	Eastleigh (70D) 2
Nine Elms (70A) 9	Nine Elms (70A) 18	Nine Elms (70A) 21	Nine Elms (70D) 14	
King's Cross (34A) 1			Weymouth (70G) 7	Weymouth (70G) 5
			Nine Elms (70A) 2	Nine Elms (70A) 6
			Guildford (70C) 11	Guildford (70C) 14

Above: No 73004 at Derby shed in 1954. Note that the original 'chime'-type whistle is still fitted. *Colour-Rail* (BRM1639)

associated with the class. For example, Caprotti versions appeared in the sheds at Aberdeen, Stirling and Motherwell. Wrexham (Croes Newydd), Carstairs and Wakefield acquired a small number of Walschaerts-fitted locomotives for the first time.

By January 1968 the remaining locomotives were allocated to two depots: at Patricroft there were 21 and two at Bolton. With the closure of Patricroft in July 1968 the last remaining Standard Class 5 (No 73069) was moved to Carnforth until withdrawal August 1968.

Routes

Like many classes the Standard 5 was associated with specific routes and workings even though the class was common across much of the BR network.

To rationalise the maintenance of the Caprotti examples, they were 'block' allocated to a small number of sheds, initially Shrewsbury and St Rollox, but the Shrewsbury examples were exchanged for Walschaerts types. The Caprotti locomotives went to Patricroft (Manchester) and became a common sight on the North Wales coast line operating alongside the ex-LMS Class 5 locomotives fitted with Caprotti valve gear.

The Scottish-based locomotives could be regularly

seen on passenger trains to Dundee and Aberdeen, and also between Glasgow and Edinburgh as well as on the Highland main line.

The batch of locomotives at Shrewsbury were used on all types of work, including express passenger trains between Shrewsbury and Crewe, Shrewsbury and Chester (Paddington–Paddington), on Shrewsbury to Hereford and Shrewsbury to Wolverhampton services, and stopping trains from Shrewsbury to Stafford, and the Central Wales trains between Shrewsbury and Swansea were also pulled by Standard Class 5 locomotives. The allocation at Shrewsbury were also used on freight services over all these routes.

In the mid-1960s during the summer months a Wolverhampton to the south coast Saturday train would leave behind a 'Black 5' (from Oxley shed) and return behind a Southern Region Standard Class 5 from the south coast. As the train ran only on a Saturday the respective locomotives would be 'stranded' at the away shed for a

Above: No 73091 in ex-works condition at Derby, April 1963. The cylinders do not appear to have been lined out. The lining on the footplate valance is a single line in Swindon style. *D. B. Swale / Colour-Rail (BRM1689)*

week before the return service. Both shedmasters at Oxley and Bournemouth would use the 'foreign' locomotive to work on any service. The author saw No 73083 *Pendragon* around Shrewsbury and Wellington and a 'Black 5' was used on Bournemouth to Waterloo services. In 1965 on the first summer Saturday services No 73087 *Linette* was seen leaving Oxford heading north with a Portsmouth to Wolverhampton service. No 73087 would have worked through to Wolverhampton.

The class appears to have been popular on special train workings, the Southern Region locomotives being seen on special trains to the (then) recently opened Coventry Cathedral.

Repair locations

In BR days standard classes allocated to regions received repairs at designated workshops associated with that region. In the early 1960s this orderly arrangement changed with the closure of many works and the need for

BR to share out steam repair work to the remaining workshops. This was not helped by some workshops being earmarked for diesel 'new build' thus reducing steam repair capacity even further in some areas. The result was that locomotives could now travel long distances for repairs, probably one of the more extreme examples of this being a 'Jinty' 0-6-0 tank stationed at Crewe South being overhauled at Darlington works in 1965, even though Crewe works at that time was still overhauling steam. Similarly the responsibility for the remaining Stanier 2-6-0s passed from Horwich to Swindon to give steam work to Swindon whilst the works were being run down. By this time all new diesel build work was concentrated at Crewe, Derby and Doncaster.

Derby. Along with Cowlairs it was one of the two designated works for repairing the Caprotti-fitted BR Standard Class 5. This work was later transferred to Crewe and Darlington in 1963 when Derby ceased steam repairs, although as noted below, the odd example of a Caprotti locomotive appeared at Eastleigh.

Crewe. The shed handled only a small number of Standard Class 5 repairs, but following the closure of many of the other works in the mid-1960s it took on more work on this class. Crewe also became responsible for

Above: No 73118 *King Leodegrance* fitted with a BR1F tender as were a number of the class allocated to the Southern Region. The number on the cab side has the larger 10in (25.4cm) numerals. The water treatment indicator is shown below the number. The tender totem is of the type used before 1957 even though the locomotive was named in mid-1959. *Ian Allan Library*

LM-based Caprotti repairs in 1963 (with the closure of steam at Derby) and later that year Nos 73127, 73128 and 73135 were seen at Crewe. However, when the author visited the works in February 1965 there was not a single example of a Standard Class 5 despite there being numerous 'Black 5', '8F', '9F' and 'Britannia' class locomotives. At this time Eastleigh, Cowlairs and Darlington had many examples of the Standard Class 5 going through works.

Cowlairs (Glasgow). This shed was responsible for Scottish Standard Class 5s. In the mid-1960s England-based examples including BR green-liveried examples were repaired there (Nos 73026, 73035 and 73096 in 1965). Cowlairs was also one of only two works designated for repairs to Caprotti locomotives (the other being Derby). The last Caprotti locomotive to be overhauled was No 73144 which received attention in April 1966.

Doncaster. Steam repairs ended in November 1963.

Darlington. This works became responsible for the overhauls of the Standard Class 5 in September 1963 following the impending closure of Doncaster works (November 1963). A change of policy required the moving of some steam overhaul work from Crewe (to allow the

Region	Intermediate and Heavy Repairs	Light, Casual and Unclassified Repairs
LMR	Derby (up to September 1963)	Crewe, Horwich, Rugby
Scottish	St Rollox (1953 to 1958) Cowlairs (1956 to 1966)	Inverurie, Inverness
Western	Swindon (to the end of 1962)	Wolverhampton, Caerphilly, Oswestry, Worcester
Eastern	Doncaster (to November 1963) Darlington (September 1963 to mid-1965)	
Southern	Eastleigh (mid-1964 to mid-1966)	Ashford, Brighton

Above: No 73000 is seen in its original livery complete with red line at both the top and bottom of the footplate valance. This lasted only a few weeks and was changed to a single red line with a grey line edged with cream used on all other members of the class. *C. C. B. Herbert / Colour-Rail (BRE1629)*

building of diesels) and Derby (closed for steam repairs from September 1963) to Darlington and Eastleigh. Standard Class 5 locomotives from other regions were overhauled at Darlington until mid-1965 and the works closed in February 1966. Caprotti locomotives No 73130 and No 73133 were observed in 1963. No 73132 was there in 1964.

Eastleigh. As with Darlington, Eastleigh only became responsible for Standard Class 5 overhauls from mid-1964 when some steam work was moved from Crewe. With the closure of many works for steam repairs such as Wolverhampton (February 1964), Derby (September 1963) and Horwich (May 1964), Eastleigh appears at this time to have been the major works for the class. As an indicator, in a three-month period in 1965, eight members of the class were observed in the works (Nos 73033, 73111, 73113, 73115, 73118, 73016, 72092 and 73093). No distinction was made as to Caprotti locomotives and certainly Nos 73126 (in December 1964) and 73133 (in 1965) were both overhauled at Eastleigh. This would have raised a few eyebrows and

caused some scratching of heads amongst the valve setters!

Wolverhampton. The last steam locomotive repairs were completed in February 1964, but this works was not extensively used for Standard Class 5 repairs. However a number of the class did receive a major overhaul including Nos 73037 (1960) and 73093 (1960). Both were painted in lined BR dark green passenger livery. At this time both locomotives were allocated to Shrewsbury and Wolverhampton was located much closer than Swindon.

As with a number of steam classes Standard Class 5 locomotives could be seen at other works usually for non-classified or emergency repairs. Examples include:

Brighton No 73049 (1955) and again in 1957.
Stratford
Caerphilly
Oswestry

The works used for these non-classified repairs were usually close to the depots to which the locomotives were allocated thus avoiding long trips back to Crewe, Swindon or Doncaster for only minor attention.

Withdrawals
Despite the fact that most of the Standard Class 5 locomotives were only a few years old, withdrawal began in the mid-1960s. The Eastern Region was the first to

Above: Many of the locomotives allocated to Scottish sheds working for the Highland main line (Eastfield, Perth etc) were fitted with brackets to allow the fitment of a small snowplough. *Ian Allan Library*

Below: Two Standard Class 5s (Nos 73030 and 73031) were fitted in 1952 with Westinghouse air pumps for trials with air-braked coal trains on the Midland main line. No 73030 is at Derby in 1953. Note the air pumps on the smokebox and the large airtank below the footplate. *Ian Allan Library*

Above: St Rollox shed in Glasgow had a sizeable allocation of the Caprotti version of the class. No 73150 is at St Rollox shed in May 1964 having been allocated there from new and was only transferred away to Stirling a month before withdrawal in 1966. The repositioning of the lubricators to behind the middle driving wheels on the Caprotti locomotives is clearly visible. Note the revised drive mechanism to the lubricators from the rear axle. *Ian Allan Library*

withdraw No 73027 (February 1964) when the locomotive was only 12 years old. Most withdrawals took place at a depot but some entered works for an overhaul but were then withdrawn before the locomotive received repairs. No 73116 actually entered Eastleigh works for an overhaul but was withdrawn at the works. This presumably was the result of a major problem being identified when the locomotive was inspected before the repairs commenced. This was not an unusual occurrence during the early 1960s. As an example a 'Jubilee' class locomotive was observed partially stripped for overhaul at Crewe but was withdrawn when major cracks in the mainframe were identified. Similarly a '9F' suffered the same fate when also at Crewe.

From that date on a small number of Standard Class 5 locomotives were withdrawn every year either because of costly repairs or that traffic requirements had changed. It should be remembered that from the late 1950s onwards BR was steadily losing freight traffic of all types to road hauliers. The last operational Standard Class 5 locomotives were withdrawn from Carnforth shed (Lancashire) in July 1968, with the remaining BR steam fleet (some 'Black 5s' and 'Britannia' class No 70013 *Oliver Cromwell*) being withdrawn a few weeks later in August 1968.

Disposal

The class survived until February 1964 by which time a change of policy by BR resulted in the majority of surviving steam locomotives being cut up at private scrapyards rather than in BR workshops. This resulted in only two BR Standard Class 5 locomotives being scrapped by a BR workshop. No 73027 was scrapped at Swindon works in early 1965. In 1967 one locomotive (No 73170) was actually cut up in the goods yard at Weymouth, Dorset by a private contractor.

In total 19 private scrapyards dismantled Standard Class 5 locomotives with six of them taking just one locomotive each. Only four scrapyards achieved double

Above: No 73087 *Linette* in lined BR black livery. The Southern Region water treatment indicator is below the number. The power classification above the number is a plain '5'. Eastleigh works painted this as 5P/5F. *Ian Allan Library*

Below: No 73134 on a murky day at Manchester, Easter 1968. The front smokebox number is missing and the shed name has been painted on the buffer beam. The top lamp bracket has been repostioned on the smokebox front. The locomotive was withdrawn a few months later in June 1966. *Author's collection*

figures but three of the larger yards accounted for 42% of the total of locomotives scrapped.

Cashmores, Newport 75
Cashmores (Great Bridge) 25
Motherwell Machinery, Wishaw 18
Cambells, Airdrie 10
Buttegieds Newport 4
Wards, Beighton 2
Birds, Risca 3
McLellan, Langholm 3
Mc Williams, Shettleston 4
Shipbreaking Industries 4
Birds, Bridgend 2
Arnott Young, Carmyle 2
Drapers, Hull 1
Arnott Young, Troon 1
T. W. Ward, Kilmarsh 1
J. Friswell, Banbury 1
Wards, Killamarsh 1
Cashmores, Weymouth Goods Yard 1

Above: No 73068 is seen at Swindon shed displaying the fully lined BR green livery applied at Swindon works to Standard Class 5s allocated to the Western Region. The red route indicator used on the WR is visible below the number. This was not applied to all the green-liveried locomotives.
Ian Allan Library

In many cases the locomotives were scrapped at a yard reasonably close to the last depot. Some moved long distances, with locomotives withdrawn from Patricroft being moved down to various scrapyards in South Wales.

No 73069 had the melancholic distinction of being the last BR steam locomotive to be scrapped at Cashmores of Newport. Having been withdrawn from service in August 1968 and following six months in storage No 73069 was towed to Newport for disposal and was finally cut up for scrap in February 1969.

A small number of Standard Class 5 locomotives, Nos 73082, 73096, 73129 and 73156, ended up in the safe haven of Woodhams, Barry Island, South Wales. All of these locomotives have been preserved.

No 73111 is seen being re railed. The numerals are the larger 10in (25.4cm) type and the power classification above the number is 5MT. The lining on the cab side is very close to the edge (common on locomotives built and overhauled at Doncaster). Locomotives painted at other works (Crewe, Derby, Eastleigh, etc) had the lining further in from the cab side edge.
S. C. Townroe / Colour-Rail (BRS1215)

Above: No 73107 in the early 1960s. Note the larger numbers usually applied at Scottish works and sometimes at Eastleigh. The AWS 'bash' plate is visible behind the front coupling. *Ian Allan Library*

Below: No 73141 at Birkenhead (Woodside) with a passenger train to Chester. At this time the locomotive was at Patricroft shed, having arrived from Rowsley in mid-1965. No 73141 was withdrawn in July 1967. *Ian Allan Library*

Above: No 73026 at Shrewsbury shed. The locomotive is fitted with ATC. Note the air pipe running under the running plate valance. For reasons not known to the author, the majority of the BR Standard Class 5s painted in BR dark green at Shrewsbury did not carry the WR route indicator below the number. *Ian Allan Library*

Below: No 73131 after overhaul at Crewe works. The lining is not quite at the edge of the valance. This allows the line to clear the small cutaway over the Caprotti valve chest. *Ian Allan Library*

Right: No 73094 at Gloucester shed in BR green livery complete with overhead warning flashes which were fitted from the early 1960s. There is no WR red spot route indicator on the cab side. The tender is a BR1C.
Ian Allan Library

Below: No 73134 was originally allocated to Shrewsbury (along with another nine Caprotti-fitted locomotives) but subsequently was moved to Patricroft (Manchester) in September 1958. No 73134 remained there until withdrawal in 1968.
Ian Allan Library

Below right: No 73144 is seen at the exit from Patricroft shed in Easter 1968. This was when the Caprotti locomotives allocated to the shed were only a few months away from being withdrawn from service.
Author's collection

The remains of No 73022 at Cashmores (Newport) yard
in October 1967. The partly dismantled firebox shows the
generous water and steam space which contributed to the
free steaming of the class. A large number of the class
(75) were cut up at the Newport yard, including the last
Standard 5 to be scrapped. *Ian Allan Library*

CHAPTER SIX

Preservation

In the eyes of the author Standard Class 5 locomotives were an elegant addition to the rail network. Four have been preserved and have been restored to traffic. Three of these were at one time allocated to Shrewsbury and were seen regularly by the author.

A total of four of the class have been preserved and a high proportion of these have been restored to traffic.

Three of the preserved examples were at one time when in BR service allocated to Shrewsbury and were seen on a regular basis by the author.

Some websites of interest include:
http://www.73082-camelot.com. The website for the group owning No 73082 Camelot.
http://www.73156standard5group.co.uk.
The website for the group owning No 73156.
http://www.midlandrailwaycentre.co.uk/73129/home.html
. This is the site for the support team of No 73129.

Conclusion

Like all BR Standard classes, the Standard Class 5 received an initial mixed reception from locomotive crews, as by nature footplate men were very conservative and would view any new class not designed on their particular railway with suspicion and compare them to the classes with which they were familiar. Once crews got to grips with driving and firing and made small changes in technique to get the best performance the Standard Class 5 was regarded favourably. The region that appreciated the class the most (SR) did not have a class of locomotive to compare, with unlike the LMR with the 'Black 5' and the WR with the 'Hall' class. It would be fair to say that many of the WR sheds with a Standard Class 5 allocation would have preferred a 'Hall' class locomotive but WR footplate crews were suspicious of anything not designed by the

Great Western Railway at Swindon. The reception for the Caprotti-fitted locomotive was more mixed but Scottish footplate crews certainly got on well with them as did footplate crews at Patricroft. The Caprotti locomotives were particularly suited to the fast flat North Wales main line, which was served by Patricroft shed.

At the end of steam traction the Standard Class 5 was still capable of high-speed running. As an example, in 1967 (on the penultimate day of steam operation) No 73097 (ex-Shrewsbury but allocated to Patricroft) averaged 60mph (96.6kph) with a six-coach passenger train between Shrewsbury and Gobowen, near Oswestry. The reality was that the BR Standard Class 5 was vastly outnumbered by the original classes of the Big Four (LMS 'Black 5', WR 'Hall' and LNER 'B1') to have a real impact on British Railways, but the class did achieve all that was expected in terms of reduced maintenance costs and availability. In the eyes of the author Standard Class 5 locomotives were an elegant addition to the rail network.

Above right: The Caprotti cam box which is driven from the centre axle fitted by a return crank with the LMS-style four-bolt fixing. Note the substantial nature of the connecting rod. *Author's collection*

Right: All the BR Standard Class 5s were fitted with roller axleboxes. Shown is the wheelset from No 73156 whilst undergoing restoration at Loughborough in 2007. *Author's collection*

Number	Built	BR History	Location (as of November 2012)	Comments (as of November 2012)
No 73050	Derby	Bath Green Park, Llanelly, Shrewsbury, Agecroft, Patricroft. Agecroft, Patricroft Withdrawn July1968	Peterborough	Nene Valley Railway, In lined BR mixed traffic black livery. In traffic
No 73082 Camelot	Derby 1955	Stewarts Lane, Nine Elms, Guildford Withdrawn June 1966	Bluebell Railway, Sheffield Park, East Sussex	Restored in BR mixed traffic black livery and red-backed nameplate, it returned to service in 1996. The locomotive remained in service until 2005 when it was withdrawn for a major overhaul
No 73096	Derby 1955	Patricroft, Shrewsbury, Gloucester, Oxley, Nuneaton, Croes Newydd, Patricroft Withdrawn November 1967	Mid Hants Railway, Alresford, Hants	The original BR1C tender replaced in preservation by a copy of a BR1G. Painted in lined BR dark green. Withdrawn for boiler overhaul in 2011
No 73129	Derby 1956	Shrewsbury, Patricroft Withdrawn November 1967	Midland Railway — Butterley, near Ripley, Derbyshire	Fully restored in BR mixed traffic black.
No 73156	Doncaster 12/1956	Neasden, Sheffield Millhouses, Sheffield Grimesthorpe, Derby, Neasden, Leicester GC, Woodford, Cricklewood, Leamington, Tyseley, Bolton Withdrawn November 1967	Great Central Railway, Loughborough	Early in 2012 the locomotive was part way through a full restoration; the wheels have now been placed back in the frames; the tender is being restored

Left: The cab side of No 73082 in preservation shows a number of Southern Region touches including the use of 5P/5F above the number as applied by Eastleigh works. The circle below the number indicated that water treatment equipment is fitted. Author's collection

Right: No 73082 in steam at the Bluebell Railway. Note how the running plate valance has been cut away to clear the face of the lubricator as an aid to maintenance. Author's collection

The Caprotti examples had the two lubricators relocated between the middle and rear driving wheels. The drive mechanism from the rear axle is clearly visible. On the Walschaerts examples the lubricators were driven from the expansion link. *Author's collection*

Left: The top of the boiler and firebox on No 73096. The steam manifold used on all Standard classes is on the top of the firebox. This would have been located in the cab on designs from pre-BR companies. The BR-style clack valves, for feeding water into the boiler, are visible. The large 'chime' whistle mounted behind the chimney was not originally fitted. When No 73096 was built the whistle was mounted on the top of the firebox. *Author's collection*

Above right: The original tender for No 73096 was a BR1C high-sided tender but in preservation a BR1G-style tender has been fitted. Note that the locomotive lacks the second vertical handrail. A replacement handrail is fitted to the tender. The square sandbox covers are clearly visible on the top of the running plate. *Author's collection*

Left: The majority of the class were fitted with the Smith-Stone speedometer. This was mounted under the driver's cab as shown in this photograph. From No 73030 the equipment was fitted from new and many locomotives built without it were subsequently fitted with the speedometer. The battery box for the AWS equipment is visible under the cab. *Author's collection*

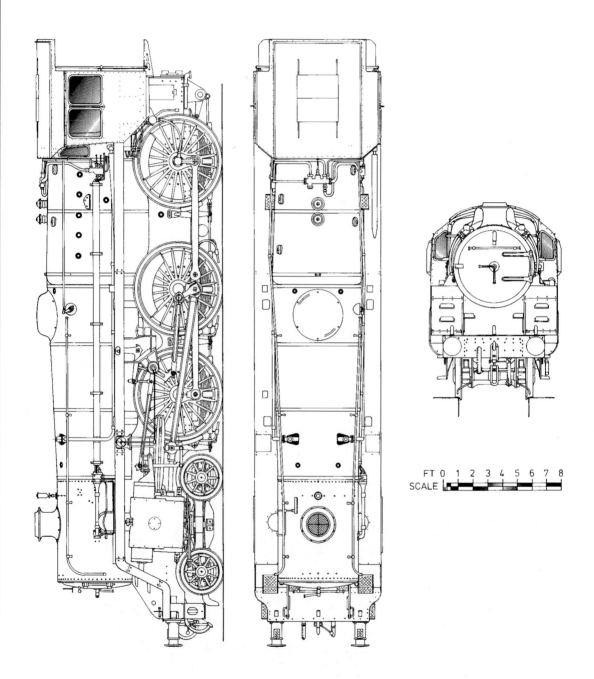

FT 0 1 2 3 4 5 6 7 8
SCALE

BR Standard Class 5, 4-6-0 Walschaerts Valve Gear
© Copyright 2008 Ian Beattie

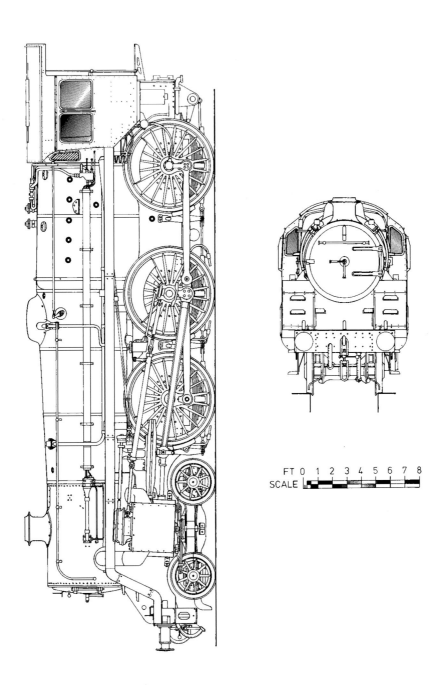

FT 0 1 2 3 4 5 6 7 8
SCALE

BR Standard Class 5, 4-6-0 Caprotti Valve Gear
© Copyright 2008 Ian Beattie

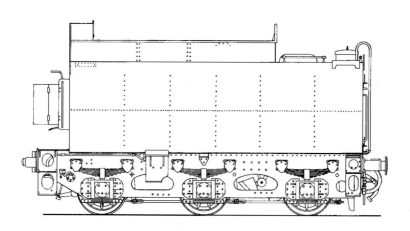

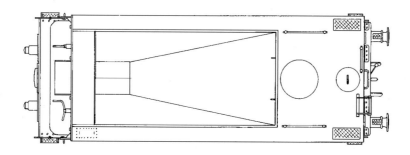

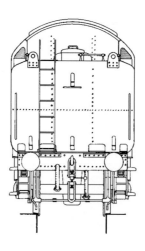

BR1 Tender
© Copyright 2008 Ian Beattie

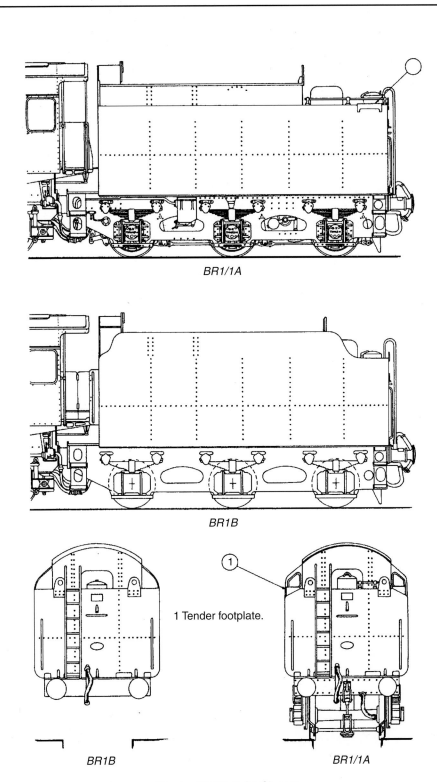

BR1/1A

BR1B

1 Tender footplate.

BR1B

BR1/1A

Standard Tenders for Class 5
© Copyright 2006 Mike Peascod

Above: A detailed view of No 73096 preserved on the Mid Hants Railway (Watercress Line) at Alresford, Hants. *Author's collection*